What Ot

"In my 30 years of hospice work, I have seen the comfort that it provides to families during the toughest days of their lives. What I did not realize was how much it would impact my own family and me. If it were not for hospice, we would not have gotten through the death of my son and daughter.

A Hospice Heart captures every emotion one goes through on this journey. It is a beautifully written book that will leave you feeling the true love and joy that can be experienced during one of the toughest times of life."

Jerene, *CEO of Hospice of Arizona*

"Terry's words and stories are impactful, heart-warming and show her true servant's heart. She is an angel on earth to all of her families and patients and will forever be ours."

The family of one of Terry's Hospice Patients

"No one wants to go into hospice! My husband was no exception. He was not ready to call it quits. Being part of hospice put him at ease. Terry answered his questions and addressed his doubts. He was at peace when he passed."

Cora, Wife of one of Terry's Hospice Patients

"With a meticulous eye for detail and a sensitivity for spotting the sacred in every day, Terry Mills, like a ghost from A Christmas Carol, takes our hand and invites us to stand silently at the bedsides of the dying and observe their final rites of passage. *A Hospice Heart* is a beautiful catalog of departed souls."

Kim Porter, *Writer*

"Terry's talent, combined with true compassion for her hospice patients and families, make her the perfect person to tell these stories. Emotional, funny, heartfelt and inspiring – you will come back to these stories again and again."

Dora, Counselor, Teacher

"Breathtaking and beautiful! This exquisite memorial honors those who have passed and will inspire you to live every day to the fullest."

Rebekah E. Ahlsten, *Writer*

"In our great desire to understand our existence on earth, A Hospice Heart: The Painful Journey to Joy confirms love as the end experience of all reality. In her touching and exquisitely written collection of stories and insights of the deeper meaning of a life lived fully, unique to itself, Terry Mills captures the essence of each person and celebrates their time on this earth."

–Rev. Dr. Hilda Villaverde,
Author of "Living on the Other Side of Fear"

A Hospice Heart

The Painful Journey to Joy

TERRY E. MILLS, LMSW

A Hospice Heart
The Painful Journey to Joy

Published by:
Terry E. Mills
Phoenix, AZ
(480) 204-1566
hospiceheart2018@gmail.com

Terry E. Mills
Telephone: (480) 204-1566
Email: hospiceheart2018@gmail.com

ISBN: 9781792838095

Editor: Terry E. Mills with Rebekah E. Ahlsten
Cover Designer: Rebekah E. Ahlsten
Interior Book Layout: Terry E. Mills with Rebekah E. Ahlsten

Every attempt has been made to properly source all quotes.

Printed in the United States of America

DEDICATION

This work is dedicated to the hospice patients and families I was honored to serve. They were -- and remain -- gifts of immeasurable joy. I owe a debt of gratitude to each. Simply put, I was touched, moved, lifted, and educated by the most gracious and generous population with which one could hope to be associated.

To the hospice team: you work tirelessly to serve the unique and individual needs of the dying.
It is a bittersweet journey.

Hospice moments are:
Precious, private and personal; they are a privilege.

To Mama: I miss your physical presence but catch glimpses of your spirit every day. I feel your love and support. Thank you.

It is with humble appreciation that I say,
"I have a hospice heart."

With respect!
Terry E. Mills
June 2020

CONTENTS

	Introduction	1
Ch 1:	The Philanthropist	5
Ch 2:	The Loving Seamstress	9
Ch 3:	The Marathon Man	13
Ch 4:	The Butterfly Man	15
Ch 5:	Miss M	19
Ch 6:	Mr. and Mrs. S	23
Ch 7:	Green Eyes	25
Ch 8:	Hummingbird Lady	31
Ch 9:	The Gentleman	37
Ch 10:	The Irish Lass	41
Ch 11:	Staten Island Queen	45
Ch 12:	The Proud Mother	49
Ch 13:	The Registered Nurse	53
Ch 14:	The Foster Parent	57
Ch 15:	The Ordinary Woman	61

Ch 16:	The Coworker	65
Ch 17:	The Veteran	69
Ch 18:	Ron, the Talker	73
Ch 19:	Mr. S	77
Ch 20:	The Free-Spirited Grandmother	81
Ch 21:	The Parents	87
Ch 22:	Rula	93
Ch 23:	The Grandchildren	97
Ch 24:	The New Yorker	101
Ch 25:	Patrice and Saul	103
Ch 26:	The Golf Pro	105
Ch 27:	The Jewish Mother	109
Ch 28:	The Military Man	115
Ch 29:	The Mexican-American	119
Ch 30:	The Couple, S and A	123
Ch 31:	Miss Tate	129
Ch 32:	The Forgiven Man	133
Ch 33:	I Took Some Time to Grieve Today	137

INTRODUCTION

This book was created by insatiable desire. It was carved into being through unforgettable experiences. I was compelled to write it to honor those who selflessly shared a profoundly personal process. I was led to this endeavor like a sapling reaches for the sunlight. It was, in hindsight, a natural process and outcome.

These pages contain small pieces of multiple journeys into uncertainty. The paths of these patients determined the content. I wrote their stories through my lens and from my experience, using pseudonyms to protect their privacy. I was happy to meet them where they were, without judgment. My goal was service while holding open a space and providing a loving presence. Undoubtedly, these experiences increased the size of my world, exponentially. This book and these stories are not meant to be devoured but slowly savored.

Love Will Survive Outside Every Box

I don't want to complain
I've been so blessed
my life has really been good
I wasn't prepared for life's end this way
I didn't plan like I should.

There were so many things
I never imagined
so many events, unforeseen
and even so, I may have thought to myself
"That will never happen to me."

From mother and father, to college
then to marriage, children and more
life sped past and the years went too fast
and now death is here, at MY door.

I'm ready to face this; I'm ready to go
I'll not fight Him to gain one more day
but there is some regret, expectations not met
some words I'd still like to say.

God only knows why I waited so long
I could've shared these thoughts long ago
I guess I thought I'd have more time
perhaps, I thought death would be slow.

It's harder to face this life every day
when death's staring you straight in the eye
perhaps I was afraid to tell you these things
in fear of this final goodbye.

So, with all that in mind, know that I've cherished
this life that tastes bittersweet
know that I love you forever in time
your love -- in my heart -- I will keep.

Know that my life was a journey of hope
experienced in unparalleled ways
know that my flame's been extinguished for now
but will be rekindled someday.

Please, do not underestimate love
by the notion that love has an end
its power complete, love will not know defeat
on life -- love does not depend.

Love will survive outside every box
love won't be bound by form or by flesh
love will live on, though the life may be gone
to love -- DEATH IS NO TEST!

THE PHILANTHROPIST

She was a well-known philanthropist. According to her husband, "She's done a lot of good." When we met, she was in the beginning stages of actively dying. She had all the chemotherapy and radiation her body could take. She was extremely weak and had not eaten in days. She was thin, her abdomen distended, and her body was essentially hairless. She wore, what she called, "a chic turban." She spoke in a soft whisper. Her husband had a high-powered job. She said, "He is always on the clock." The money was unlimited, but time was scarce. He came to the unit as time allowed. She said he was a "workaholic." Work was his coping strategy all his life, especially now.

Although my name is Terry, Nadine called me Karen. She was in a lot of pain. She did not like to wake up alone. We spoke of death, dying, planning, family, quail, bunnies and the golf course surrounding the unit. It was a beautiful place and she loved the picture window. We laughed and cried together. We sat in silence with her hand resting in mine.

She had good friends. They would call or come to my office and ask for Karen. I would say, "I am Karen, but my name is Terry." That was confusing. I explained that Nadine called me Karen and when I corrected her, in the beginning, she had forgotten. So, Karen, I became. Nadine asked her friends to check in with Karen, and I could update them, as needed. Her friends were grieving her inevitable and approaching loss. She said, "Soon they will know that death is the best option, but not yet."

In a few short days, she became unresponsive. Her eyes were open and would track movement in the room, but she could not respond. She would hold a gaze with penetrating green eyes that begged for attentive presence. When I could, I sat with her. I would leave the room when her spouse or visitors arrived. The other staff also helped with a visiting vigil and kept her company as she slowly and silently drifted away. Nadine was the first in a long line of hospice patients, for whom I wrote a poem. Her husband asked if I would read it at her memorial service.

The service was huge. She touched so many lives with her philanthropy. When it came time to read the poem, I stepped to the podium and introduced myself as, "Nadine's Hospice Social Worker, Karen." Nadine taught me a powerful lesson: My job is not about *who I am*. It is about *what I do*. I am service.

In Her Eyes

In her eyes she's telling me a story.
In her eyes she's showing me a sign.
In her eyes I've seen her days of glory.
In her eyes: I've seen her slow decline.

On her face I see her fight to linger.
On her face I see her try to stay.
On her face I see her time is nearing.
On her face: The hope of one more day.

Dying is not what she's afraid of.
Dying is not what keeps her here.
She is bold and willing to move forward.
She is holding on, but it's not out of fear.

It's for them – sitting at her bedside.
It's for them – she's hesitant to leave.
It's for them – she's holding on to moments.
It's for them – she hates to see them grieve.

She'll hold on until she's sure they're ready
She'll hold on until they've found their peace.
She'll hold on until she knows they're steady.
She'll hold on until their doubts have ceased.

THE LOVING SEAMSTRESS

She was 79 years old and transferred to our hospice unit from the hospital. She had actively begun the dying process. She was a wife, a homemaker, a mother, a grandmother, and a seamstress. She loved her family and her dogs.

As a young wife, she was excited to travel and was always an interested observer. She enjoyed looking out windows and enthusiastically reporting what she saw. She was a joyful cook and a strong moral compass for her children. She and Tim lost a son early on and developed a sincere gratitude for life – committed to living it -- to the fullest.

When we met, she was close to death. Tim felt encroached upon; he was torn. He wanted more time but did not want to see her suffer. He said they "talked about this" and he was given "orders." He agreed to let her go without "heroic measures." He struggled with that promise. I told Tim that respecting her wishes *WAS* a heroic measure. The following poem was written on the day she died; it was their 54th wedding anniversary.

Myriam and Tim

54 years today, since the day
these two were hitched.
54 years of life since they
first became bewitched.
Myriam and Tim were wed
and became a family --
blessings were bestowed
on these new parents of three.

Lots of travel, lots of friends
and lots of love and fun
sororities, interfaith
and needlepoint well done.
The furry kids: Fido, Royal
Mac and little Herb --
were sweet companions
romping through a life superb.

Derrick is a good boy
their grandson turning ten
his mom is, "all girl,"
and she is very feminine.
Aunt DJ, a tomboy
but still an Irish Lass --
with mischief in her eye
and endearing Irish laugh.

Retirement and then
some special years together
time to mend some fences
and face a change in weather.
Cancer struck and took a hold
on Myriam, so dear
now Tim has a heartache
and in his eye, a tear.

The last six months have been hard
Myriam has suffered
Tim has been her advocate,
through him, strife's been buffered.
Somedays she would say to him
"Tim, I need your help --"
and Tim would not give this up
or be anywhere else.

This anniversary
as Myriam's life is fading
there are loving arms, I know
patiently awaiting.
Arms that are strong enough
to hold her loved ones tight --
as we celebrate the wondrous gift
of sharing in her life.

THE MARATHON MAN

He was sixty-five when he died in our hospice unit. His wife described him as "determined." He was successful in business, a loving husband, and a devoted father. He was resilient, flexible and humble. He believed in hard work. He ran nine marathons and participated in almost 2,000 Volksmarches, in all fifty States. He was generous and thoughtful until the end. "Play the hand you are dealt," he would say. His love for his family and friends was NEVER doubted and was evident in his family's love and devotion. His wife was clear about his prognosis and impending death, yet struggled with the harsh reality facing them, "It all seems so surreal." She would ask, "What is happening?" His two daughters' sadness was profound. Their lives were shaken by the sudden inexplicable illness, (acquired abroad on a family vacation) that rendered their dad weak and frail. It was too much for them to absorb. As they sorted through anticipatory grief, and since they missed home and their dogs, I arranged for a pet visitor. It was heart-warming to watch them hug the accommodating Collie and shed their tears into her soft hair. It was a small comfort in the midst of a huge loss.

A Different Kind of Marathon

He's running a different kind of marathon
it's just this race has been so long
and though he's tired of this pace
he's connected to this place
and he's hesitant to stop running and move on.

Because he shares a love that's truly rare
and his family has always been right there
so he is hesitant to go
he's been strong for them, you know
the thought of leaving is hard for him to bear.

So, as he reaches yet another finish line
and he knows he's running out of time
he'll leave a legacy of love
and he'll be watching from above
'cuz in this race – he'll leave no one behind.

I have a hospice heart.

THE BUTTERFLY MAN

He grew up on the East Coast. After graduating high school, he went straight into the military, where he became an officer. At one time, he was an Olympic swimmer. His best swimming event in competition was the butterfly stroke. He was a talented cook and a contented fisherman. His little sister, (the kid), who was sixty when I met her said, "He didn't know a stranger."

When she was called by the hospital and informed of his massive stroke and grim prognosis, she caught the first flight to Arizona from New York. She was eager to share their story. Her brother always said she was, "a force to be reckoned with." I spent time with her each day. She had adult children in New York, who loved their "Uncle Earl." The stroke left him unable to speak, or swallow. He was minimally responsive but managed a slight, half-faced smile when he heard her voice. When she walked into the room, his face lit up. She could absolutely brighten up the darkest day. It was good that they got to be together for his good-bye.

Out in front of our facility, up on a pedestal, there was a bronze statue of a little girl. Her arm was outstretched and reaching up. On the tip of her finger, was a butterfly. His sister said that he was called the "Butterfly man," by the senior community at the pool. She said, "I knew he was in the right place when I saw the butterfly."

Earl and the Butterfly

He was born in Pennsylvania
went to the University of Penn
then straight into the OCS
'cuz they needed our young men.

He became a captain
he was a dapper kind of gent
he lived a life comprised of
Love and time well spent.

He was a fisherman, an adventurer
a swimmer, and a cook
he was as comfortable with a spatula
as he was with rod and hook.

From New Orleans to Sedona
and horseback rides to cruises
Earl and "the kid" would share
the bumps of life and bruises.

Now as the end draws near
they are here together
to face the trial of their lives
in this patch of stormy weather.

But with a smile on her face
and a light within his eyes
they've found comfort here
underneath the butterfly.

MISS M

She was 99 years old. She was from the Deep South, a devout Southern Baptist, and a faith-filled woman. It was her faith and her family that carried her through the pain and fear of approaching death. She smiled and said she had, "A good friend in Jesus." She became forgetful. She said that after all the time she spent in The Bible, she was now afraid she would forget "The Word." She feared her recollection would fade away, as so many memories had. Each visit, we went through a Bible verse; it soothed her.

As she progressively and rapidly declined, she was confined to bed. Her family members became around the clock caregivers. She began to see people that none of us saw. One day she said, "Step out into that hallway and see who that is." I turned as if there would be someone there. She asked, "Who's comin' yonder?" I saw no one. She shouted with delight, "Oh that's my brother. He's been fishin' and lookey; he's bringing me some fish (she slapped her knee). He brings me fish every day." I asked, "Are they bass?" She looked at me with frustration and asked with conviction, "Can't you see them is perch?"

Endless Love . . .

Endless love is what you have
as this life comes to its end
I know you'll be looked after
by our mutual Jesus friend.
He'll lead you through golden gates
you'll hear the trumpets sound
and His Father will embrace you
as another lamb, now found.

He'll take you in His arms
and hold you close and deep
as your loved ones rejoice
and shed their joyful tears of grief.
They'll miss your presence here
and your tender, thoughtful ways
but they know you'll come
to greet them at the end of earthly days.

Though parting is deep sorrow
because love was true and strong
you'll soon be resting in His arms
the place where you belong.
You'll share stories of all of those
who cared for you each day
and God will smile on them too
and give them gifts of Grace.

Yes, you've been led to your Lord
and you're leading them to Him
it is yet another gift
you have proudly given them.
They will always remember you
and they'll keep your love alive
because by design -- and in God's plan --
endless love survives.

I have a hospice heart.

MR AND MRS. S

I worked with a couple in their 90's who had been married for 70 years. They were both their parents' only child and they never had children. They chose, instead to travel. They made good friends along the way, who had all, sadly died. They said that losing friends was one of the drawbacks of a long life. They were all each other had. As I visited with them toward the end of her journey, they shared that they had taken a shower together, "Every single day," of their married life! "EVERY DAY?" I asked, shaking my head, in disbelief. She abruptly said, "EVERY DAY, for Christ-sake." I looked at him; he shrugged and said, "We saved water." We all laughed – it was a moment of private honesty, priceless recollection, and pure love.

As she grew weak and unable to stand in the shower, he adapted the shower and put in a seat. He added grab bars for himself, so they could shower together as long as possible until she was bedridden. He remained by her side, stroking her hair and looking through albums of pictures of their travels. He refused a hospital bed because he wanted to sleep next to her until she died.

As the Years Go By

As the years go by and I reflect
so many memories fill my heart
with sweet regret
of those who touched my life
and now are gone
I must admit – I wrestle with the effort to go on.

In days gone by how we shared such times
from marriages, to babies born
to our friends' decline
and though a tear may fall
as life grows dim
I find comfort in remembering all of them.

As the years go by and I reflect
my heart is VOID
of any sadness or regret
because I've lived a life completely full
and I've had the chance
to share my life with you.

GREEN EYES

He was in his early 50's, with long, dark hair and green eyes. His skin had a yellowish tone. His wardrobe consisted of two pair of jeans and a few t-shirts. He was living in the home of his departed parents. His sister had died in that house, as well. Because his dad was his employer, he had not paid the mortgage or any other bill since his dad died almost two years prior. The City turned off the electricity and the water. I was unable to get them re-established. The Sherriff's office had come by several times to serve eviction notices, which Green Eyes ignored.

He never paid into Social Security; never paid taxes. He lived outside of the system. Now, as a result, the system was not there for him. He was a self-proclaimed "loner." He had pancreatic cancer that spread to his liver. He had adopted three strays and bartered for dog food. He sold family items, clothing, and furniture for money for occasional fast-food, bird-seed, and laundry (he only had one load). He had a few homeless friends who would stop by to look in on him.

He had two daughters he never met. He knew where they were and that they were fine and "all grown up." He declined the inpatient unit, because of the dogs and his few friends did not have cars. In light of the eviction notice, I found him another place to live, or rather die, at no charge. They would allow the dogs. He said, "My family died in this house; I want to die here too." He did not want to die around, "a lot of strangers." So, we got him a prepaid phone to call us or 911. It struck me that the phone plan included 70 minutes of talk-time -- more than he would need.

I brought a few non-perishables from the food bank, every other day. His appetite was poor. The RN and aide visited twice weekly. After her first visit, the RN took his laundry home and brought back three new shirts. The aide bought soap, a bucket, and a two-gallon bottle of water at the dollar store so that Green Eyes could bathe. We filled a bin of water for the dogs, from the neighbor's hose.

On the day he died, I arrived with non-perishables. He was unresponsive. His friend said he had been that way "all morning." I called the

RN, who called the aide. The RN and the aide bathed, shaved, and changed him. He remained unresponsive. I spent time with his friends and provided end of life information, which he and I arranged through a donor program, at no charge. His three friends each agreed to take a dog. When I left, I knew I would not see him alive again. He was lying on the couch, in his favorite place, facing the window. He had freshly laundered clothes; combed hair and a clean shave. He was in no pain. He was clean, safe, comfortable and cared for.

The Sheriff arrived with the final eviction notice, stating that the premises had to be evacuated "TODAY!" His friend told the officer that Green Eyes was dying, and hospice was attending to him. The officer drove away. Green Eyes died several hours later. His friend used the cell phone to let us know. The story was over and as per the eviction notice, the premises were evacuated. Dying with dignity means different things to different people.

End of Life Issues

There's a box to check and a note to write
that indicates when someone is dying.
There's an imminent assessment to ascertain
if the family is appropriately crying.
There are booklets to give and papers to sign
there are e-mails to send and there's more
you musn't forget, it isn't done yet
till you've sent the appropriate grief score.

There are phone calls to make, discussions to have
and arrangements must be completed.
There are face sheets to update (and you need
somewhere to synch) if anyone's going to read it.
Then you must "verify," you've documented it all
as accurately as you are able
and prove to your peers you are up to the task
and each day, emotionally stable.

Then go to the meetings and tie on a ribbon
that shows you somehow got through it.
Tell a brief story then move on to the next
because it's the only way you can do it.
The checkboxes fail to show by a click
how you personally managed to make it
and most of the time, when it comes to the loss,
I quickly check, "Not evaluated."

The assessment of what I've been recently through
needed notes in the comment box.
And I had to take five and regroup for awhile
until the ache in my heart – just stopped.
I clicked on dismayed
I clicked on afraid
I even clicked on confused
I wrote in a note
with a lump in my throat
that simply said, "I miss you."

I have a hospice heart.

HUMMINGBIRD LADY

She was 94 and lived alone. Her biggest concern, at my first visit, despite her diagnosis of oral cancer was that she was becoming too frail to tend to her hummingbirds. I put in a referral for a volunteer. Two weeks later . . . still no volunteer. She was distressed. I offered to come by every week until a volunteer was found.

Our visits began with the cleaning and maintenance of the feeders, (under her watchful and supervisory eye, of course). She gave me specific instructions, which I followed, closely. The food was previously prepared and adequately cooled by the time I washed out the feeders and scrubbed off the debris. There were three, as well as an upside-down garbage can lid that doubled as a bird bath. I scrubbed that too.

In her younger days, she was a "Socialite; an Aristocrat." She had traveled the world with her spouse and was wise to the ways of the aristocracy. She was polished. She was a proper lady of status. Now, she had good days and bad days. She was thin and gaunt; she used a cane in the house, a walker outside, and a wheelchair for distances.

Due to pain, she could not eat. However, she forced herself to drink 4-5 cans of a meal replacement every day. She was more than embarrassed (mortified) because the cancer tumors in her mouth and throat caused her to spit when she spoke. She carried a neatly folded tissue at all times to wipe her chin and lower lip. I told her not to worry, "Sometimes, I spit too." Our laughter united us.

She kept travel journals, from 1952-2005, including photos of every trip she had taken. I suggested that we read the journals. It was a way we could share her personal narrative, without talking. We traveled together by plane, train, limo, and ship. We shared Spain, Hungary, China, Japan, Taiwan, all of Europe (she broke her ankle in London). She made such good friends along the way. We looked over ship manifests, airline tickets and fares. We read about the treasures she bought, the meals she savored, and the times she got lost while exploring -- how she loved Tuscany.

Now, each morning, she forced herself to get out of bed. The pain was worse and required more medication. Still, she would meticulously dress and be ready to meet her public with all the flair she could muster. She was impeccable.

Physically, she was declining. She walked less and tired more easily. She was losing weight. Swallowing became more difficult. On one visit, she shared her extreme fatigue. In light of her declining status, I asked if she would consider staying in bed? She looked at me, perplexed. With certainty and sarcasm, she blurted out, "No!"

As she continued to decline, I kept up my weekly visits. I tended to the birds. I read the journals when she was unable to sit with me, but dozed in a chair close-by, holding my hand. Until now, she had not thought about an "afterlife." She believed that life well-lived -- with positive intent -- was important. She believed in goodness, hard-work, and family. Self-sufficiency was vital and paying your own way. She asked me on several occasions if she should feel guilty that Medicare was paying the costs for hospice. I reassured her.

She now had 24/7 caregivers. She and I were at the kitchen table. Her gaze was questioning. She did not know what to expect. She said, "God should hand out punch cards. That way you would know when your time was up." She said, "You would know then if you should go on that cruise or have that $6,000.00 dental procedure." Her sense of humor and practical nature were undaunted.

I told her no one knew exactly what to expect. I said, "I only know, we will be here." She said, "I hope so." I now visited briefly every day. She slept through my visits, only waking to hug and kiss me hello and goodbye. The RN was visiting three times a week. Our aide visited twice a week to assist, educate and encourage her private caregivers, who were not as equipped to deal with death as the hospice team. I continued reading her journals. I read them all.

Early one morning, at about 2:30, I received a tearful call from her caregiver. I was there within fifteen minutes. Mae had passed. I said her name, softly. I leaned over the bed and stroked her hair. I called her daughter, who was a proper woman of status. She politely thanked me for the call. I called the RN to visit and "pronounce." I called the mortuary. Later, as the van pulled away, I waved good-bye. I felt a deep sense of appreciation for the precious journey we shared.

Mae

Hospice was recommended
for a condition that is grave.
There will be no turning back
and Mae's life will not be saved.
She's strong and independent
she has compassion shining through
she doesn't know what lies ahead
she's not sure quite what to do.

A mother and world traveler
she's lived an extraordinary life.
A gracious blue-eyed woman
she was a kind, devoted wife.
From stone-paved paths, to plains of wheat
Hotel Eva and Beira Mar
stone Nymphs in fountains gazing on
as she ate almonds in the car.

Friends for lunch in Mallorca
a tour of the ruins in Spain
walking through the streets of Paris
or dining in on days with rain.
Fishermen in Portugal, women washing clothes
in sand and stream, Evora to Quattaria
she's kept track of all she's seen.

Her travels fill her memories
and take her to another time
when cancer hadn't found her yet
and living was on her mind.
Her children and grandchildren
are bright lights that still remain
she reflects in times of darkness
like in sleepless nights on trains.

Rossio Square in Lisbon
Rome, Italy, or Paris, France
she and Merle set out to find
the rare wisdom found in chance.
Hawaii's orchids, Tokyo's trains
The Golden Pavillion and Hong-Kong
The Phillippines and Singapore
the list goes on, and on, and on.

Now her traveling days long over
she's in bed most every day
but like the hummingbirds, she tends to
she'll soon have to fly away.
So she'll take another journey
one more trip to one more place
where she and Merle will reunite
and explore the State of Grace.

THE GENTLEMAN

He was 99 and legally blind. He lived alone in a low-income, senior housing complex. He was a Veteran of World War II. He had a bad heart. He had some strands of thinning white hair peeking out from under his cap, which he would tip whenever he said hello. He had a well-trimmed white mustache and sparkling blue eyes (the bluest, blue). He leaned forward when standing and used a walker when he left his home. He had a thin, slight build and his face was gaunt. He had a daughter, who lived in another city. She was a single, foster parent of six children. The Gentleman and daughter were not close. He said there was a "fundamental difference," in the way they lived their lives. When he received his Social Security check each month, he sent her $200.00.

I took him to the grocery store every other Tuesday for the senior discount. He wanted the "Three B's," bananas (had to be green), bread, and butter. His list also included: Cereal, eggs and Jimmy Dean Sausage. He cooked breakfast on Friday, for the manager of the complex and the security guard. He bought a lottery ticket every week. He used a cane inside his apartment. He insisted on standing whenever I came into or exited a room. He was ashamed he could not open the car door for me and embarrassed when I did it for him.

He invited me to his 100th birthday. Every widow in that complex had a story to tell. They were eager to share their part in his care; he had admirers! One day after we returned from shopping, he asked me to marry him. I sadly declined. He said, "Well it was worth a shot."

Several weeks later he had a sudden cardiac event. He was taken to our inpatient unit, where he died. I think of his blue eyes, often -- in the produce section.

The Gentleman

A blue-eyed, elderly gentleman
making his own way
he said, “I’m happy to be walking,”
on any given day.
His gentle sense of humor
his deeply wrinkled brow
his hand upon my arm
sweet memories to me now.

A sweet and feeble father
forgotten by his child
no judgment from him toward her
his manner was too mild.
Generous and loving –
he was blind -- to faults and foes
we humbly reaped the benefits
of all the love he sowed.

I have a hospice heart.

THE IRISH LASS

She was 86. She was born in Ireland and a devout Catholic. After college, she came to the U.S., with her best friend. They settled in New York. They worked hard all their lives and retired 45 years later (with pensions), each from the first job they found. She loved the outdoors and golf became her passion. They moved to AZ and they purchased a small summer home on the beach in Del Mar.

She started to show signs of dementia in her 70's. She constantly lost keys and purses. She became agitated, irritable and angry. The doctor said it was stress-related. They went to the beach house. Arm in arm they walked the beach every morning and had tea on the terrace. They found comfort in each other's company. Life was good, again -- albeit short lived. Her agitation and combativeness proved to be too much for her friend. They returned to AZ and her friend was forced to put the Irish Lass in a Group Home. They continued to visit together every day. It became clear that hospice was the next step. She had stopped eating. She lost her ability to speak. It was hard to tell how much she understood.

She was calm and quiet now but could no longer walk. She had to be fed, bathed and cared for. Her friend continued to visit. They would sit outside on cooler days. Since they had taken walks together all their lives, her friend pushed her in a wheelchair to the end of the block, before ending every visit.

Their bond began in Ireland and remained strong until the day she died. Her friend's grief was profound; she felt alone. She suffered a deep loss, in silence. She could not speak about it; she said, "Because of the religion, you know." It broke my heart to watch her bear the loss without speaking of the depth of her love and devotion.

She's an Irish Lass and Passing

She's an Irish lass and passing
from this world to the next.
She's going to her kingdom
as she takes her final rest.

Confusion's left behind her
from now on, she's thinkin' clear.
She'll be watching over Tara
her precious friend left here.

She's an Irish lass and passing
to a new and glorious land.
She's walking on another beach
still holding out her hand.

She's waiting at the shoreline
she's holding a quiet space.
Until she's joined once again
she'll be living in His Grace.

She's an Irish lass and passing
her body had grown weak.
Her mind was challenged in a way
'twas hard for her to speak.

Now her spirit lives undaunted
no longer caught inside her gaze.
There will be no suffering
and she'll not ever be afraid.

There are 60 years of friendship
that will never see an end.
She is in the ebb and flow
of the waves that cross the sand.

She's in the breeze that blows so sweet
from gate - to door - ajar.
If Tara's ever lookin'
her love will not be far.

I have a hospice heart.

STATEN ISLAND QUEEN

She was 96 years old. She was from Staten Island, New York, and an Irish Catholic. Her son brought her to Arizona after she fell and broke her hip, which could not be repaired. Pain was a constant companion. She spent a lifetime walking the streets of New York. Now, she would not walk again. She did not want to come to Arizona! Her son said she was "stubborn and ornery." I said, "You do not live to be 96 and self-sufficient if you are not!" He said she was, "used to getting her way." Now she refused to eat. He said, "We are at odds."

The day I met her, she was lying in bed, tightly squeezing her eyes closed, pretending to be asleep. I introduced myself and she remained asleep acting. I said, "I heard you have stopped eating?" She opened one eye and responded, "It's not going to happen." I asked her to tell me what that would mean? She said she would, "Probably die." I asked her how she felt about dying? She replied, "The sooner, the better." Her adult son was grunting and rolling his eyes. I asked how I could help if she had already made up her mind about death and dying? She said, "Just be my friend."

I began each day by having coffee at her bedside. I ended my day by going to her room and saying goodnight. She refused to eat and refused any liquid supplements. She was in too much pain to get out of bed. Her personal care caused excruciating moments, for which she had to be medicated. She would only drink sips of water.

She told me stories about growing up in Staten Island. We began and ended our short relationship reminiscing about New York City, Staten Island, and her family. She was a single mother, who raised her son on a small salary. She was an apprentice baker, who became a "Master Baker" at a young age. Her husband left when her son was in elementary school. She said her husband was a "drunk."

As she declined, her son stayed 24/7, sleeping on a cot in her room. She quickly became weak and unable to speak. I told her stories of trips as a youngster to New York and the magical rides on the Staten Island Ferry. I continued to have my morning coffee with her. She had a child-like smile until the very end but remained mad at her son for bringing her to Arizona. I told him the most precious gift we can give is the *Gift of our Presence*, even beyond disagreements. His mom knew her son did what he thought was right (she told me so). He was having a difficult time. I suggested that he talk to her about his feelings, his childhood, and New York memories (Yankees, never Mets).

She never wanted to, “burden him,” nor did she want him to witness her death. She said it would be “too hard for me to leave like that.” I watched the fear and anger melt away as he shared memories, tears, and laughter. I watched her forgive him. Early on a Saturday morning, her son went to get a cup of coffee. He stopped by the nurse’s station and chatted briefly with the nurse. When he returned to the room, his mom had died. She had gotten her way.

Hospice Will Be There For You

When the distance and the anguish grow
because of what one hopes and what one knows
when time is short, and words are lost
when future dreams have all been tossed.

When death is at the open door
to dash the hope of one day more
when sadness, hurt, and pain prevail
and medical efforts too, have failed.

It's time to make another plan
and find someone to take your hand
as you enter now into a place
where you're sustained alone by grace.

Our hands, we offer now to you
to help you do what you must do
to hold a place for you to grieve
as those you love must take their leave.

And to this, we add just one more thought
because we've seen the battle you've just fought
love and grace will see you through
and hospice will be there for you.

THE PROUD MOTHER

She was young, not yet 50. She had two children, who were almost grown and precious in her sight. She was funny, kind, caring and on some days, she was afraid and tearful. She knew she had a disease that would take her life. What she hated most was leaving her family, especially her children. She wished that her life had not taken this course. She said, "Nothing can be done." Several other family members died from the same illness. It was slow, progressive, painful and debilitating. Her muscles and nerves were affected. She lost her independence. She did not want heroic measures once breathing and swallowing were compromised. Her deep and abiding love for her children and her youth made these decisions extremely difficult.

She and her family were trailblazers in Arizona hospice provider services. They knew the course of this particular illness and knew its progression. Hard decisions were made as each stage of decline was encountered: No more diagnostic testing, no more aggressive therapies, no feeding tube, and no CPR.

They gathered at her bedside: family, friends, clergy, and colleagues. A vigil of sorts, with plenty of stories and lots of laughter. She died peacefully, surrounded by their selfless compassion. They let her go with love and that love led her home.

The Ultimate Gift

She was a young woman
stricken with an illness, unforgiving
an illness that stripped away abilities
for activities of daily living.
She fought the fight with bravery
and a gathering of her supporters.
She held on to her sense of humor
and she kept a stash of quarters.

She liked "Patches," baseball
and enchiladas with, "That Baja Sauce."
She liked anything that was salty
and a mocha from Starbuck's.
She watched channel ten, "The best,"
each morning during breakfast.
She liked commercials about, "Best Buy,"
her love for THEM was steadfast.

She would ask me to make a call for her
when she wanted a connection.
Her mom, children, or her siblings
would change a bad day's direction.
She loved with heart and soul
her inner child -- fought to be mature.
as she faced decline in dire days
and she struggled to endure.

The love she felt for them
was the strongest love that I had seen.
She loved them so completely
and unconditionally it seemed.
But then I saw the greatest gift
that – to her -- they had bestowed
when they gave the ultimate gift -- of love
the gift of letting go.

How selflessly they carried out
the wishes she'd expressed.
To let her leave this life on earth
and proceed onto the next.
How courageously they walked the walk
through the sadness and the fear.
Her body has moved on
but heart and soul are forever near.

I have a hospice heart.

THE REGISTERED NURSE

She was 62. She was a lifelong, full-time nurse. For the past 30 years, she lived a glamorous California life as the private nurse to a celebrity and his infirmed mother. The lifestyle afforded luxuries that she never expected. The job changed her and took her a long way from her roots. She had siblings, who did not live the way she had become accustomed. They were uneducated but possessed the wisdom acquired when living isolated and away from the mainstream. She said they were, "people who lived off the land: Hunters and fishermen." They were not particularly socialized, other than to one another. They bore a unique responsibility for the family. She supported them, financially throughout their lives, but saw them infrequently, until she was diagnosed with stage four breast cancer. She said life had so many "layers."

Their strong family devotion came to the forefront. The siblings came to Arizona, where she owned a home. The cancer spread rapidly. There were difficulties with her decision to take the "hospice highway." Family dynamics were strained. They wanted her to get well. They prayed for a miracle. Letting her go, without continuing chemotherapy, or radiation was against what they believed . . . but it was what she wanted. She was at peace; they were torn.

I watched their struggle and listened to their fears. I saw them once a week. We visited alone or with them, depending on the day. The siblings had a fundamental religious faith that was steeped in traditional beliefs. She had a loose grasp on faith but believed that she was in, "God's good hands." They began reading a book, which she would sleep through most of the time. She had read it before and believed in its message. The book was called *Discover the Power within You* by Eric Butterworth.

The cancer was aggressive, and it was spreading. Her brain was now involved; she became unresponsive. She was transferred to the inpatient unit, where she died. Her family was extremely grateful to our unit the last couple of days because those were the hardest for them to witness. She died surrounded by love; she was clean, safe, comfortable and cared for. About two weeks later, I received a package in the mail at work. It was that book and it made me smile.

The Layers of Grief

It's that time in life when loves ones leave
the day has come; it's time to grieve
we knew the reality long ago
but there's so much else we didn't know.
We never imagined the layers of grief
or the many friends now deceased
we did not consider it all in depth
sometimes, we are inconsolably bereft.

The lives, the love the memories dear
the sadness for those remaining here
the losses of those that cut too deep
the painful release of tears we weep.
The loneliness that is unexpected
the quiet thoughts in times reflective
that silent telephone that doesn't ring
the heartfelt wish for normal things.

Our age has now caught up with us
as age and aging always does
few friends remain; our parents gone
the years progress and time moves on.
Looking back with smiles wide
linger memories of those who've died
we shared such wonderful, fruitful times
now, unfortunately and sadly, left behind.

But oh, those days of glory when
we shared those laughs friend to friend
the jokes that made our tummies ache
the candles on the birthday cakes.
The weddings, the baptisms, and bar-b-ques
so many outings with so much to do
the stereos playing our music loud
the busy, bustling holiday crowds.

The smoke, the cocktails, the neighbors in
the dance, the food, the sheepish grins
the day, the time, that fleeting youth
now faded into stone-carved truth.
And time will take what time can claim
we make allowances for another change
but this I know -- and this I'll say
I'd not have it another way!

THE FOSTER PARENT

He was a family man and a man of deep faith. He had ten children, four of whom were adopted. He and his wife had fostered over 100 children in their 40-year marriage. He knew he was dying. He was not afraid. He was tearful at leaving his family but, joyful to be meeting his Brother, his Maker, his God. He was anticipating reuniting with his son, who had drowned -- and a good friend, who was taken by cancer at a very young age. He was excited about the reunions. He loved golf and considered his walk toward death a long, green fairway leading to the "18th hole."

I visited him weekly. He asked me to read scripture to him. He particularly liked Psalm 139: "Lord, You have searched me out and known me." He was certain of God's presence. His faith went far beyond words; it was unwavering. He knew his family would be, "Lifted up," by his loving and merciful God. I stood by and witnessed his wife endure, in silence. Her grief was unspoken, yet evident. His death was quiet and peaceful. I once asked him to sum up his life. He said, "It was awesome."

It is Time for Me to Let You Go

This life of unexpected gifts
and precious times of smiles
leads us to unexpected grief
and unexpected trials.
It is not that we are unaware
of things to come our way
it's just that we are not prepared
when comes that final day.

It is time for me to let you go
It's time to say goodbye
I've a thousand years to grieve
and a million tears to cry.
I'll miss your sense of humor
I'll miss your eyes ablaze
I can't believe it's true, my love
that we'll not share more days.

Death is a life completed
the end of our journey here
yet as the day draws nearer and nearer
my heart is full of fear.
I want to grasp and hold your soul
squeeze tightly onto you
that you'll not float away one day
as I know you have to do.

No, I can't bear the loss of you
I am strengthened when you're near
alone at night, I beg my God
"Can't you please just leave him here?"
Then my heart is awakened
as I hear my God's reply:
"The 'HELLO' that is waiting for him is
as incredible as this good-bye."

So let me anguish; let me grieve
let me weep and sob.
let me do what I must do
to give you back to God.
Let me miss you, let me long
let me feel the ache
so you can hear that great "HELLO"
as you enter in His gate.

It is time for me to let you go
though I am at a loss
It's time for me to think of you
no matter what my cost.
I will not fight another day
and cling to have you here
I'll let you go -- to that "HELLO,"
please know: I love you, dear!

THE ORDINARY WOMAN

She was 99 years old when I met her. She was living in a group home, where she was loved and cared for. She was visually impaired and extremely hard of hearing, non-ambulatory, and needed assistance with all activities. Her memory was poor. She liked flowers, birds, and the color aqua. Her daughter resided in California. She lived on a small farm and owned horses, which made it difficult to get away. She kept in touch by Skype. One day the daughter reminded me of her age. She said, "Afterall, I'm in my 70's, you know." It was true; I had forgotten that if my patient was 99, her children would most likely be in their 70's. It made us laugh.

When Marilyn's 100th birthday approached, I called her daughter and asked for information, so I could write a "birthday poem." I practically had to interrogate Val to create a gift of poetry, but I finally succeeded. Her daughter was ecstatic and grateful for the poem. She said, "It was perfect." She said she made copies and sent it to, "all my relatives." I was grateful I was able to give them a gift – after 100 years of an "Ordinary life."

Marilyn's 100th Birthday

An "ordinary" life, her daughter recalls
full of everyday "stuff," triumphs and pitfalls.
"Nothing special," her daughter, Val says
"We just did what was needed," with no regrets.

She was born in Chicago, as was her spouse
they grew up living behind each other's house.
Across the alley, they were "backyard neighbors"
Herman died from cancer, many years later.

"He was the Salt of the earth," Val says today
she says, "Everyone looked at him that way."
His parents, from Europe, good "Polish" stock
never extravagant; just solid as rocks.

A brother named Greg, sadly died at 33
gave Marilyn her niece, whose name is Treenie.
A housewife and mother; a daughter, an aunt
a volatile young woman, if given the chance.

Her sour kraut and spare ribs still bring a smile
even though it has now been quite a long while.
Val says Marilyn no longer remembers
how good she cooked and the joy she tendered.

Val is her good girl; she always obeyed
she grew up strong and she still is today.
Val had a child, a boy she named Scott
like Marilyn, one child is all that she's got.

An ordinary person, a normal life
nothing special, or different
just the passing of time
simple people, who simply towed their own line…

. . . nothing special
for 100 years . . .
just the passing of time.

THE CO-WORKER

She was a manager in hospice with many years of experience. She had a kind heart and a loving presence. She was a dedicated employee who never said no when asked to assist with events, meetings, meals, or planning. She raised her children alone and was single for most of her career. She was elegant and graceful, yet down to earth and appreciative of the idiosyncratic nature of others. She was accepting and inclusive.

She met a wonderful man and they married. He was a surprise she never expected. She was truly happy and for the first time in years, felt like her life was full. Their wedding was well-attended and the entire firm was elated. He became a regular face around the office and was well-liked. He, too, was a helper and a servant – but enjoyed being with her – no matter the event, job, or task. They were happy together . . .

One night, after they had returned from an office dinner party. He walked into their room and said he had chest pain. The erratic scene that transpired over the next hour was surreal. He was gone. In an instant, her life had changed. Had it really happened, at all? She told me about the "brain fog and the blur."

YES. The path our patient's walk, and upon which we accompany them, hits way too close to home. Life has a way of reminding us – that death is as much a part of our own stories – as those we serve.

One Word

No words, but one, that sufficiently say
the thoughts weighing heavy on my mind today.
No words, but one for an empty stare
stripped of a future, was waiting there.
Hopes are dashed, dreams are gone
the task too great in moving on.
A marriage brought to a tragic end
the loss of an intimate, special friend.
No words but ONE will see you through
on this path laid out in front of you.
Yes, just one word in the trials you face
you are safely wrapped in the arms of GRACE.

I have a hospice heart.

THE VETERAN

He was a young man, not yet 62. He was a Viet Nam veteran and a self-proclaimed "Pothead." He drank every day from about 5:30 pm till the bar closed. He slept till noon. He lost a leg in the war. He had a small apartment, behind the bar in which he and his friends lived out most of their lives. He told me his liver was "shot." He was not married but had three adult children, he never knew. His parents died, and he lost track of extended family. He had given up on haircuts and hadn't seen the dentist in years. His long brown hair matched his dark brown eyes. He was talkative, friendly, and forgetful. The bartender in his, "dive-bar," a young woman in her early 40's watched over her, "flock," and agreed to be his Power of Attorney (he had a big crush on her). She was married with children.

He had an amazing way of looking at the world. He was glad he had the "right" to live the way he chose to live. He said he preferred to live, "Under the radar." I couldn't help but think – as a nation – we let him down. We didn't take very good care of him when he came home from the war. Now, he was dying, pretty much alone. He knew his fate, despite the worsening confusion. He had a condition caused by his liver disease that prevented his blood from clotting; he was bleeding and had received all the blood the hospital could give him before the hospice decision was made. He said he was only on hospice because "there was no other choice; nothing could be done." He wanted to live. He was not "ready for death". He said, but "death is ready for me."

I had the honor of sitting with him and listening. He told story after story, over several days, before he simply stopped talking and peacefully left our world. I arranged for his cremation and contacted the Veteran's Administration to make sure he would have an honorable burial beside his military peers.

Drunks, Has-Beens, and Dreamers

He was lying in a hospital bed
recounting days of old.
His words rolled out softly
as he shared moments etched in gold.
He was a vet; he was a dad
he was – oh so many things . . .
and today he isn't sure what more
his humble life may bring.

The doctor said an intervention
would just "prolong" his life.
He shrugged and said, "Why not prolong
I still want to be alive."
He told me stories of all the places
he'd frequented of late.
He couldn't say the day, or time
he didn't know the date.

His words would run together
he was confused at times.
I listened as he talked to me
his eyes were glued to mine.
He had kids he didn't know
and one good friend, who cared.
He faded out for just a moment –
lost inside his stare.

There's a lounge called the, "Union,"
where he has, "a lot of friends."
He has helped some through painful times
he likes to sit with them.
He says they tell, "The same-old stories,"
each and every night.
But, "What the heck, it's ok,"
he's still glad that he's alive.

He says, "They're a bunch of drunks
has-beens, and dreamers."
They are misfits and potheads
some are thieves and schemers.
And they start their friendly gathering
each day at half-past five.
He smiles and says, "Why not prolong,
I still want to be alive."

I have a hospice heart.

RON THE TALKER

He was born in the Midwest. He married young and he and Anne lived in a modest house on the lake. They had seven children. He loved his home and grieved its loss when they moved to Arizona. The kids felt like it was unsafe for their parents to be alone in such a big house especially with Anne's increasing forgetfulness. The move was hard on Ron. He said much of his life was now, "In storage."

True to his Irish roots, Ron had the gift of gab. His wife said, "Ron can certainly spin a yarn." It was difficult to visit Ron because it was hard to leave his stories. He was kind, friendly, supportive, charitable and loving. He was forgiving. He loved deeply and could easily profess his love for others. He was a devout Catholic. He wore a Scapular around his neck and a Miraculous Medallion pinned to his shirt. He had heart disease, kidney disease, and was diabetic. Neuropathy made it difficult to walk and made him a fall risk. Hospice provided an electric scooter, which gave him independence and a better social life in his retirement community. He loved to talk to people and people liked to talk to him.

Ron spoke fondly of family members who had died, but he spoke most often about his Father. He shared many wonderful memories. He deeply loved and admired his Dad. Ron hoped to measure up to the high standards his father set. Every member of the hospice team was touched by Ron and his family. I never had a doubt that his Dad would have been very proud of the man his son became.

Oh, How I Loved My Father (For Ron)

Oh, how I loved my father
and it brings a smile to my face
as tear-filled eyes reflect upon
what time cannot erase.
From bicycles and lessons learned
to football games and talent
my Dad was strong and capable
he was sensitive and gallant.

Orphaned at the age of seven
and thirteen different moves
the man could pick a horse
who simply wouldn't lose.
A football carrying half-back
committed to the game
driving cabs with Arthur Godfrey
before he found his fame.

A handsome, freckled Irishman
rich in prose and charm
a bus driver and a dentist
who believed in, "Do no harm."
Listening to the, "Mama" song
over and over at times - a cigarette
and a beer or two, were his only crimes.

And how I loved my father
the man I miss so much
how I miss his gentle smile
and crave his loving touch.
A Catholic man of faith
and he'd tell me now today
In Christ's promise, we'll meet again
and he's never far away.

MR. S

He was in his late 90's. He did not know how old he was. He said, "I quit worrying about it." That was the usual reply when he did not know the answer to questions, which was most of the time. I learned early on, not to ask questions. He lived alone, since his wife's death, nearly ten years prior. He couldn't remember when Joan died; he had no idea if it was yesterday, or five years ago. He enjoyed a good cigar under the shelter of his huge carob tree. He basked in the sun's warmth and the company of his dog, Benji. He told me he was "Content." He did not leave the chain-link fenced front yard, unaccompanied. He said, "I know better." His disorientation, once out of his yard, was profound.

His daughter, who lived out of town, visited every month and/or whenever necessary. His son visited every Wednesday and Sunday, or as needed. They both called several times every day. He had a flip phone he kept in his shirt pocket. Sometimes his kids would call the house phone to remind him to put his cell phone in his pocket. I was taken by the haze in which he lived. I often wondered what it was like in his head? Did he think? Were his thoughts scattered? Was he at peace? Did he worry? Did he want something more? Were there moments of clarity?

He drank alcohol. He had always been a drinking man. His adult children felt it was not fair to take away the few pleasures remaining. His son bought him a quart of whiskey every two weeks. He drank to excess when he remembered to drink; sometimes he simply forgot. On most days when he drank to excess, he fell. Sometimes he could get up; sometimes he waited for somebody to come and help. His family made sure that between them and all other caregivers, their Dad was seen twice a day. He often had cuts and bruises he would laugh about. He'd say, "Oh, I don't know what happened. I always get into something."

I took him lunch every other week. He called me his, "lady friend." I did the dishes, then we would sit in the yard with the dog, under the Carob tree he and his wife planted "50 years ago." He would draw deeply off his cigar and tell me the same stories he told me the visit before. I listened and responded like it was the first time.

Mr. S, My Friend

He seems lost inside his silence
and trapped inside a gaze.
He seems cut-off, somehow
but he doesn't seem afraid.

His appetite is pretty good
he likes to take a drink.
He enjoys a nice cigar
his brain won't let him think.

His memory's diminished
his sanctuary is home.
His children are his saving grace
he says he misses Joan.

It's not the way he'd have it
it's not what he had planned.
But underneath it all
remains the dignity of the man.

I see it in his eyes
I sense it in his smile.
He's lived a satisfying life
despite the snags and trials.

THE FREE-SPIRITED GRANDMOTHER

She was in her early 70's. She was tall and slender. She had short, curly, greying hair. She was wide-eyed and clever, with a sense of humor, which was hard to match. She was always three steps ahead of everyone else. She loved to dance. She was an adept argue-er. She was so intuitive, one thought she could read minds. She was on oxygen due to her lung disease and the first thing she ever said to me was, "I am not going to quit smoking." I replied, "I would never ask you to." She said, "We'll get along just fine." Her death would be swift. She saw and felt it coming. She was not ready to go, and she was vocal about leaving too soon. When she heard I was a poet, she began telling me about herself. She said, "I have some things to say." She chose to say it through my poetry.

What an honor to relay parting words to her family. It was her final gift to me. There were things she wanted them to know and remember. I took notes and worked on the following poem. Time was of the essence. She was extremely happy with the poem and made me promise to remember her, "Love of life," whenever I read it. She said that "death," was not the important part, but LIFE was! I presented the poem to her family with her name listed as a co-author. Her young grandchildren were over-joyed that their grandma was "a poet." That was my final gift to her.

I Have Some Things to Say

You mean so much to me
my family and my friends
I have some things to say to you
before this lifetime ends.

Now in this time of crisis
with six months or less to live
I don't want to leave you yet
when I've so much more to give.

So these words will help me tell you
some things I have to say
and I'm hoping these words comfort you
on that approaching day.

When my precious Lord and Savior
reaches out His loving hand
and leads me on a journey
to another special land.

You know me as a fearless friend
never one to be afraid
and I'm not fearful now
in this bed, my God has made.

I have been so blessed, you see
throughout this life so dear
and you have deeply touched my heart
on my adventures here.

I have been a whimsical woman
I have had a lot of fun
square dancing and traveling
always kept me on the run.

I divorced my husband, Jon
then I married him again
the second time around
we grew into better friends.

God has lifted and transformed me
my faith today is strong
His love is real, and I am sure
I had a guardian all along.

Blessed with my three children
Myra, Jim, and Shawn
it was easy for me each day
to find the reasons to go on.

My blue eyes are still shining now
as I face what lies ahead
because I know that I live on
that no part of me is dead!

My grandchildren and grand-pets
may shed a tear or two
but don't cry long, 'cuz life is short
and there are so many things to do.

I leave a legacy of joy
I've merely moved to another place
where I'll be surrounded by His love
and I'll be living in His grace.

And I know that we will see each other
in another time
'cuz I live on in your hearts
and you will always live in mine.

I have a hospice heart.

THE PARENTS

Sometimes in this work, the challenges are insufferable. There are no “Perfect” solutions. Circumstances lead us to difficult choices, of which none are satisfactory. The struggle becomes palpable. The powerlessness feels unfair. Tears are sometimes the only effective coping tool in the moment, yet the relief is fleeting. Tears do not move us closer to solutions, but surrender is a necessary part of moving forward.

Stella was 63 and the only remaining daughter of a couple in their very late 80’s. She lost her sister, in a horrible car accident. Now, she missed her more than ever. She said she was, “Mad” at her sister for not being there to help. I understood the struggle in the lack of solutions facing this wonderful, loving family. Unfortunately, I had seen it too many times.

Stella’s mother was our hospice patient. Her dad was declining as well. Both parents were weak and frail. Stella’s mom had Alzheimer’s and had to be watched at all times. She was unsafe due to forgetfulness, a tendency to wander and she was a fall risk. Stella’s Dad would lead his wife around by the hand. He showered her and changed her. He put her to bed each night and got her up each morning. She had stopped eating and was having trouble swallowing liquids. Stella would help when she could (a little every day), but her husband was disabled and needed her too. She felt pulled in every direction. She was exhausted. She said things would be, "So much easier," if her dad would, "Just agree to move." She said moving was, "Their only choice."

Her parents were never wealthy. After the hospital bills, there was no money left. Their only asset was their home, which was paid off years ago and in which, they had equity. No amount of persuasion would get them to sell and move into a group home setting. Her Dad said, "We have lived in this home for 40 years and we will die here." There was no money for paid caregivers. State assistance would take time to put in place; most-likely, more time than her mom had. We had a family meeting and Stella told her dad that moving was, "The only way to do this." Her dad looked at her with tears of kindness in his eyes. He said, "I disagree." He went on to tell her that he and his wife had the “right to live and die the way we choose.” He said they had a “right to live an imperfect life and die and imperfect death, and life had never been perfect.” He said, “Struggle is nothing new.” Stella relinquished control that day and surrendered to the struggle.

It's My Right

Life becomes quite complicated
and goals become unrealistic.
If only life were predictable
and one could plan logistics.
Mother cannot remember me
we never thought to plan for that!
My sis passed away at 53
and I've still got her cat.

If sister was here to help me
I am sure we would find a way.
But dad can't help; he is past that point
he says, "I've out-lived my days."
The hospital bills hit hard each month
they never really saved.
Their checks cover what they need
we can't account for what they gave.

They can no longer live alone
it is their impossible dream.
Without money, without assistance
there is no way out it seems.
Dad assures me they'll be "Just fine,
and don't worry, I'll watch the wife."
He doesn't know he's incapable
and his words cut like a knife.

He's worked so hard; he's been so good
and now his days are winding down.
He wants to be left alone with mom
the way it has been till now.
How can I respect his wishes?
Tell me, how can I sleep at night?
When they might just die alone at home
he says, "Honey, it's my right."

I have a hospice heart.

RULA

She wore oxygen. She had a bad heart and her lungs were compromised. She could walk short distances, with a walker. She needed assistance with, "Anything that requires wind." She had limited endurance. She was a devout Christian. The connection she felt in fellowship had a healing power. She said it was the reason she could be happy in her decline. Her daughter was a flight attendant but kept in close contact with her mom. Rula always knew where her daughter was and when she would visit, next. A Pastor visited Rula every week for communion and other leaders in the church, visited regularly.

The group home in which Rula resided kept a regular staff, with regular hours. Rula liked and needed the consistency. She was very well cared for by loving caregivers. She used to tell me about life on the farm in the Midwest. She marveled at how blessed her life had been. She would tell me at every visit, "You don't have to look too far to see the hand of God." She always had a grateful heart.

God's Hand for Rula

She's in her 90's now
and she's doing fairly well.
She says she misses doing things
now that she is frail.
She sleeps a lot and eats a little
she is happy where she lives.
She says that she is blessed each day
by all that "Jesus" gives.

She has a love for Jesus
that carries her through each day.
She likes it when I visit
she has so much to say.
She is hoping I will join her someday
in that sacred place.
Where we will know God's tenderness
and feel His warm embrace.

The care home is a pleasant home
and caters to her needs.
Her daughter visits often,
bringing books, clothes, and treats.
She has so many friends from church
who come almost every week.
She says, "I'm so grateful."
There's nothing more that I could need.

Her eyes are blue and tearful
when she shares, "the Word," of God.
She "Ministers," to me
when she shares her loving thoughts.
She says one thing that is clear to her
and easy to understand
Simply put, in her words
"It is easy to see God's hand."

THE GRANDCHILDREN

He was eight years old. The little ones are innocent on this journey, with life lessons looming large. Death is an unexplored reality that will be deciphered by their experience. Death is as much a part of life as breathing, yet it is feared, loathed, thwarted and avoided. Why? Normalizing death has a way of lessening its power. A deep understanding of the endless power of love and being able to convey that, can mean the difference between unbearable heartbreak and "appropriate grieving." Understanding death can transform extended heartache into normal coping, as death becomes a matter of course.

Children know – their wisdom has not been altered by years of attachment. We can learn about the realities of life and death through the eyes of our children. Loss is hard. Death is not. We weep in loss. What would happen if we honored death like a diploma, a graduation of sorts? Scripture says, "Grief will last for the night, but joy comes in the morning." Love and life should be our focus; death and dying serve to ring in the celebration.

I Held a Child as He Cried

I held a child as he cried
he was snug against my chest.
His grandpa had moved onward
to take his final rest.
The boy was broken-hearted
his mom was crying too.
He was just too young
to know quite what to do.

I saw it in his eyes
that deep and real concern.
So many truths lie up ahead
so much more to learn.
I stretched my arms out wide
he leaned closer into me.
I held a loving place
was safe for him to grieve.

Without a word of wisdom
without a fitting phrase
he lingered in my arms
while I escaped his gaze.
I felt his beating heart
I felt the loss he bore.
Holding him was all I had
I could do no more.

As I held him in my arms
now afraid to let him go
afraid he'd ask for answers
I can't pretend to know.
He leaned back and said
"I'm hungry, can I eat?"
I let out a breath
and got him ham on wheat.

I got the boy some milk,
a napkin and a chair.
He ate and drank his milk
while I was sitting there.
They thanked me for the visit,
the pop and sandwich tray.
No words were lost between us
there were no words to say.

I still feel his beating heart
and the wetness of his tears.
Now, I can see the wisdom
in all his 8 and one-half years.
Hold me and I'm hungry is all we need to say.
Being held and being nourished
help us through each day.

THE NEW YORKER

Tina was all her daughter, Beatrice, had. Beatrice said, "We've always been together." They came to Arizona from New York as the result of a transfer. Beatrice would not have taken the promotion if Tina was not in agreement. Tina had lived her entire life in, "The City." She walked the streets of Manhattan every day. Her favorite place was Long Island. She squinted on sunny days, peeked out from under an umbrella on rainy days and layered with wool underneath a slicker, on snowy days. Rarely, would weather keep her from a walk. Tina loved the city. She loved New York and being a New Yorker. The culture, the pace, and the people suited her.

They lived a satisfying life in Arizona. They were both involved in community activities and loved Arizona's version of the Theater. They enjoyed walking through their suburban neighborhood. They called it the "Countryside." The quail, the cottontail, the birds, geese, ducks and even the coyotes became part of their walks. Tina died in our unit, after a two-year battle with cancer. It warmed Beatrice's heart to think that her mom had returned to the city.

Tina

July 20th, in the year 2007
just after - noontime -
Tina returned to heaven.
She ended a long journey
but she left some folks behind
who will mourn her precious loss
I'm sure, for quite some time.
But her life has been a battle
in these last few trying days
overshadowed by some sadness
and a painful kind of haze.
So as we say goodbye
and we console all those who grieve
we know that others see her coming
as we tearfully watch her leave.

. . . And somehow now, I can see her smilin'
as she enters a crosswalk in Long Island . . .

I have a hospice heart.

PATRICE AND SAUL

Patrice was from Bolivia. She was granted, refugee status, in the U. S. at the age of 16 and given a work visa. She was adopted by a family In New York, through a local church and assisted with a job as a clerk at a large phone company. That's where she met Saul. He was a nice man. He was a simple man. He was polite and kind and somewhat shy. One day, after he had known her for about a year, he asked her to dinner.

After 30 years both retired from the phone company and moved to Arizona. Ten years later, she was facing his death as cancer ravaged his body. She was sad. She said she never felt as alone, yet she was immensely grateful. She was his caregiver, his wife, and his only love. He was her, "Savior in many ways," she said, "He gave me a normal life," at the age of 18, when she had no idea what was to come next. "What more could I have asked for?" She wanted me to know, remember and relay -- what a gift she received in Saul.

Your Life was Blessed by Loving Saul

From Bolivia to the United States
from the East coast to the West
you've come to trust your God and know
that He knows what is best.

Through the grief and through the pain
the love you shared with Saul remains
through the tears and through it all
your life was blessed by loving Saul.

Every prayer was answered
God gently listened in
and He was there with you and Saul
until the precious end.

Through the grief and through the pain
the love you shared with Saul remains
through the tears and through it all
your life was blessed by loving Saul.

THE GOLF PRO

She moved to Arizona from the East coast to retire in the sun. Every day, she and her friends would golf or visit the tennis courts, senior softball diamond, or pickleball court. They hiked, rode ATV's and traveled together – all 8 of them. But she and Rae had a secret that was never disclosed to the others. It was, "just too personal," and their generation was, in many cases, "adverse to that."

Their retired lives revolved around as much fun, as possible. She was their trip planner. They were always on the go. When I became acquainted with the group, Linda was dying. She and Rae had decided not to go the aggressive route, knowing the outcome would be the same. Linda said, "Why go through that, when terminal, means terminal." Rae was sadly supportive.

As the end grew near, she was never left alone. They would take shifts or gather together. They would laugh, tell stories, talk about current events, or sit quietly and read, knit, do needle point, or play cribbage. What fun they had together as they celebrated Linda's journey. I was honored to witness such a tribute to friendship.

Her Game was Under Par

They gather at her bedside
as her time begins to fade
she's surrounded by their love
and the memories that they've made.

They've hiked and golfed and traveled
they've biked and ATV'd.
now they're keeping up a vigil
as they approach the time to grieve.

She made a hole in one once
but nothing can compare
to the sweetness of the memories
and the eight who will be there.

From the driving of the school bus
to the photos of the owls
she's the social director
for the outings of her pals.

And we must remember Betty
sister's struggles are profound
Linda will be there for her
she's never let her down.

And one thing I know for sure
is that this nurse anesthetist
with every Putt, or Birdie
will be cherished long and missed

As she reaches those golden gates
though the journey may be far
the gates will swing wide open
because her game was under par.

I have a hospice heart.

THE JEWISH MOTHER

She was in her mid-nineties. She was slight of build and frail, with big brown eyes and beautiful white hair. She was from New York and kept her East coast accent. She was widowed. She had one daughter, who was loving and involved. Esther said that when she was a girl, she always wanted to be a "Jewish mother." Esther's words were kind. She was appreciative of what others did for her and eager to say, "Thank you." She had suffered a massive stroke and needed assistance with all activities. She was hard of hearing and legally blind. She had to be placed in a Group Home.

Her affect was flat, and until you got to know her, it was misleading. She was able to interact, participate, and answer questions appropriately, if given time (and it did not involve memory). She was good IN THE MOMENT. She needed time to process what she was responding to -- and time to form her words. Time had become a luxury of which few people had enough, especially caregivers with multiple patients. Her care was excellent, and the setting was beautiful. However, oftentimes, caregivers had moved onto the next task, before Esther was able to interact. I sensed her frustration. I wanted to give her time. Most of our visits were an hour. She would say, "Oh please come again. I feel so much better when you come; you lift me up so high." I saw her every week, but she did not remember. I told her that I looked forward to our visits and she was a highlight in my week. Her face lit up and she would ask, "Really?"

She liked to pray and sing hymns. We started our visits with prayer from the Old Testament, or the Psalms. Her favorite was Psalm 61. After our prayers, I played the hymns on my phone and we sang along: "I Come to the Garden Alone; How Great Thou Art; The Lord's Prayer; Somewhere Over the Rainbow." She said the rainbow song was, "My favorite hymn." It made me smile. I am not a good singer. My mother told me in an Irish brogue, "You couldn't carry a tune in a bucket." But if my patient wanted to sing, then sing we would! Once after singing our hymns, she said, "Next time maybe we could sing louder and better." I said, "I know I could sing louder, but I am not sure about better!"

When she died her daughter asked me to come to the graveside service. The Hospice Registered Nurse and aide attended, as well. A harpist played softly throughout the memorial. The Rabbi facilitated, and it was beautiful. As the service ended, Esther's daughter went to the front of the group and announced that I would be singing, "Somewhere Over the Rainbow." I almost fell out of my chair. Nervously, I said to the group, "I am sorry, I do not sing -- I sang with Esther -- but I do not sing." Feeling on the spot, I asked if I could say a few words? I proceeded to tell the group how Esther had touched me and what a blessing it was to serve her. I told humorous stories about our visits. The group's laughter was resounding as the harpist softly played, "Over the Rainbow." I knew Esther would have loved it. I felt her presence and could hear her saying, "That is my favorite hymn."

Esther

She was generous with a compliment
her words were always kind
although you often had to wonder
what was on her mind.
She'd welcome you with open arms
as if none other ever lived
she made certain that you knew (to her)
you were, such a gift.

She could convince a wolf, or snake
they were the kindest little dove
when you were in her presence
she would make sure you felt loved.
Yes, the sweet woman was hard of hearing
and she could barely see
but I was worth a million bucks
when Esther looked at me.

She sang, she prayed and thanked her "God,"
for the blessing's He bestowed
she eagerly spent her fruitful life
reaping what He sowed.
She was grateful when she woke
to be alive another day
yet she believed she'd meet HIM soon
and clearly see his face.

No longer blind, no longer frail
and now able to hear Him speak
no longer tired, now transformed
to strength again -- from weak.
Esther's in the garden surrounded by
birds and plants and flowers
She's saying of the sunshine
"I could sit out here for hours."

I have a hospice heart.

THE MILITARY MAN

He was devoted, to any cause in which he believed. He had strong opinions and was not hesitant to voice them. He had a sense of humor that provided laughter to any gathering. He was a fun guy to be around, when he was a fun guy to be around. He was strong and healthy most of his life. Lung disease eventually caught up with him, most likely from his military service and where he was stationed. That place claimed many of his fellow servicemen. He loved his family and appreciated the support they offered as he reached the end of life. His wife held a sweet place for him in her heart and always will. I facilitated a short memorial service at the Veteran's National Cemetery. The Military Guard, the multiple gun salute and Taps took my breath away. When his nephew presented the flag to Rubright's wife, it was all I could do to hold myself together. My heart was stirred by the love and honor he was shown. I have kept in touch with his wife, who is doing well as she begins a new chapter in life. I asked her if I could rename his poem and include it in this book. She said I could leave his name. I am happy to . . .

Rubright

A military man who served
more than twenty years
proud of his service
and his military career
if asked how long he served –
he'd tell you tongue in cheek
"I was in for twenty years" –
and he'd add, "plus one week."

From Germany and Florida
Hawaii and much more
two tours in Viet Nam –
he never spoke about that war.
Returning home, a sergeant
still calling all the shots
well . . . his family says . . .
"at least that's what he thought!"

He made it to retirement
and poker games at 3:00
enjoying day trips in the
desert and riding ATV's.
A close group of crazy friends –
with happy hour at 5:00
enjoying life's many gifts
and glad to be alive.

He was a father, a husband
a friend and just a hoot
he was honest to a fault
it'll be hard to fill his boots.
Hilarious by nature,
coming up with funny things
to make his family laugh
in the turmoil that life brings.

Adjusting to some heartaches
and obsessing over news
all the kids were warned
not to share political views.
And a smile will come around
where you are today
if you think of Richard Rubright
and his simple, loving ways.

So as we close this chapter
and begin another book
we can see our traveler
explore heaven's every nook.
No oxygen tank to mess with,
no cough and no disease
and no damn toll highway,
or pulling over just to pee!

THE MEXICAN-AMERICAN

His name was Juan. He was homeless. He was malnourished. He had end-stage liver disease due to cirrhosis. All his possessions were stolen on the streets and he had been badly beaten. He had no ID. His family had lost track of him. We came into contact due to a necessary hospital discharge and nowhere for him to go. He was able to speak in a quiet whisper. He was Spanish-speaking. He said that his family had "Plots" for burial in Mexico – his home. He was Catholic. He asked that he return to Mexico to be buried. Time was of the essence. Through a long paper trail of medical records, we were able to locate a nephew, who lived in a one-bedroom apartment with his son and fiancé. Juan's nephew took Juan in and was able to reach Juan's estranged daughter in Texas. She came to AZ to help with the care of her dad and to meet him for the first time.

Since Juan had no ID and no income, it was difficult to plan his trip to Mexico. His mother and sister lived there and were anxious to receive him home, if we could get him there. I contacted the Mexican Embassy and an Arizona State

Representative. I explained his circumstance and dying wish to be buried in his homeland. I contacted an organization called, "The Bucket List Foundation (BLF)." Through the efforts and cooperation of all these agencies, Juan's wish came true. The Arizona State Representative worked with the Mexican Embassy to confirm his identity and provide proper papers. The Embassy visited Juan at his nephew's apartment for photos and an ID was issued. Juan was escorted to Mexico by a volunteer, Spanish-speaking nurse, on a flight that was paid for through the Bucket List Foundation. BLF also arranged for an RN to meet him on the Mexico end of the flight. Juan's daughter accompanied her dad to the airport to say a tearful goodbye to the father she had met just months before. Juan died less than two months after returning home. He was buried next to his father.

A Mighty Guardian

When life was at its bleakest
and the future seemed quite dim
I am convinced he was walking
with a mighty Guardian.

The timing was essential
all things had to fall in place
if his final wish would be granted
it would require Grace.

The family came together
all the agencies stepped in
his mom and sister made arrangements
for his journey's end.

Juan lived to meet his daughter
and he made it home to die
and his wishes were fulfilled somehow
beneath a watchful eye.

I have a hospice heart.

THE COUPLE, S AND A

They were married upward of 60 years and both in their late 90's. It was the second marriage for both of them. They shared 16 children. They were from Montana and farmers all their lives: Hard-workers, resourceful, able and creative. They were fundamental Christians and raised their family to be the same. S said that he liked to, "Worship in Truth and in Spirit." He liked a Spirit-filled celebration. The religious services in the facility were too, "Calm and quiet," for his taste.

He said he missed the, "Open spaces," in which they grew up. He and A now resided in a one-bedroom apartment on the second floor of a senior-living retirement facility. They didn't leave the building. He said they were, "Self-contained," and now that hospice was involved for both of them, they didn't have to leave the building for doctor's appointments. He said, "It works out."

S was growing forgetful and it worried him. A's dementia was advanced, and S was A's eyes and ears. She needed him to remember -- for her. He wrote things down. He kept calendars in every room. They went to the dining room for three meals a day. He used an electric scooter and she was pushed down in a wheelchair, by facility staff. He ordered off the menu, but A ate the same meals for breakfast, lunch and dinner. It didn't seem to matter. Her dementia was too far advanced. S was grateful that his precious A could still sit up at the table and eat with him, and that her swallow was not yet compromised. She no longer remembered how to use silverware. He often said, "She was the best wife." She was once a talented seamstress. She made much of the children's clothes and all the vests he wore.

They sat beside one another in, "lift," recliners. She slept most of the days away. He, too, dozed in his chair. She could not walk but could stand and pivot to get from chair to Wheelchair. His arms were weak and he feared on some days they would not be strong enough to lift his Bible. He could walk short distances with a walker. He would say, "Yes," with each step. It was a way of affirming that he could do it; falling was out of the question.

My visits were from 10:00-11:00, on Monday mornings. It was a wonderful visit and a great way to start the week. Each visit began with a conversation about what had transpired since my last visit: Who had visited, how services were on Sunday, contacts with the hospice team, and if S and A had eaten that morning. That conversation usually included a brief account of my hour drive over: The hawks, the weather, the traffic, the blessings in the day and the gift of my time with them. They wanted Scripture read to them and S kept track of where we left off each week. It was a pleasure to share such sacred time with these wonderful people.

S and A

I wonder how I could describe
the essence of these two
kindness permeates from them
and their love is pure and true.

Their eyes are full of joy –
yet a hint of sadness lingers
she no longer sews because
she can't control her fingers.

He's happy with TV
he tunes in to favorite preachers
he believes in their wisdom
he looks on them as teachers.

But he'd like to drive a tractor
or cinch a saddle's strap
take a walk out in the cornfield
or in the sun, a nap.

He'd gaze upon what's golden
and enjoy the endless green
he'd walk across the farmland
there's so much for him to see.

From the number on his door now
down to the dining room
if he loses sight of gratitude
he'll be touched by gloom.

He's content and he is blessed
with what the, "Lord provided"
He'd never tell his children
somethings he has confided.

But if there was a way to stay
at home down on the farm
They'd be there now and stay there still
despite weakness in his arms.

MISS TATE

She was in her mid-90's. She had the end stages of Alzheimer's dementia. She did not move voluntarily; her joints were constricted. She could not walk. She could not tell you what she wanted or needed. She had to be fed, bathed and transferred. She was alone with the exception of an elderly niece, who had her own challenges and could visit only infrequently.

Miss Tate resided in a group home where she was well-known and well-cared for. The home was always clean. The food was always fresh. The atmosphere was calm and quiet. I saw her and the other residents every two weeks for a half hour poetry reading. They were happy participants. Miss Tate sat quietly in her wheelchair. I made it a point to make eye-contact with group members and was surprised that if Miss Tate was awake, she was looking directly at me. I could, at times, sense her presence; perhaps in a fleeting moment of clarity. I always hugged and kissed her hello and good-bye and she would make a pleasant sound, like, "hmmmmm?"

One particular day, as I finished the poetry and was leaving, I hugged her and said, "I'll see you later, Miss Tate." In a clear and strong voice she asked, "Where ya' going?" We all gasped – she was there. Everyone applauded, and the group home staff lit up. It was a precious moment. Life is a series of precious moments; is it not?

I Knew So Little About Her

I knew so little about her
there was no info from her past
and no answers to the questions
I wished that I could ask.

Did she ever bear a child
and was she married at one time?
Where had she attended grade school
and what was on her mind?

Did she always have a sweet tooth
and did she like to be outside?
Were her parents from the valley
was she glad to be alive?

Was she comfortable and cared for
and was she brave or was she scared?
Was she abandoned by her family
or did she feel they cared?

And although I could not ask her
I was never compelled to try
'twas enough to hug her hello
and share a hug good-bye.

THE FORGIVEN MAN

He was 74 years old when he died. He was a mechanic until he retired at the age of 62. As a young man, in the early 40's, he was a baker onboard ship for the U.S. Navy. He was an artist and genius with his hands -- a talented carpenter. He was resourceful, creative, intelligent and proud. He was a Pisces and loved to be around water. He was a swimmer, skier and boat pilot. He liked to think of himself as a "carouser." He had an eye for the ladies and it was evident to anyone who paid attention.

He was married with four children. He met his wife in the Navy in 1946. She adored him. He drank and smoked to excess. His wife died in 1984 after 37 years of marriage. He then remarried to a family friend, 16 years his junior. Somewhere in this timeline he fathered another child who was raised in her mother's family, never knowing about her real dad (my dad), until shortly before he died. All his children were unaware, because honesty required accountability. Lung disease claimed him after several brutal years of breathlessness.

Dad

My dad, he died in hospice
he was not a very nice man
he raised the four of us:
Timmy, Val, Me and Anne.
We were at his bedside
at the time he passed away
at the old Bryant's Center
very early in the day.

Since that time, I've seen him die
a hundred times or more
that face, those eyes, that heartbreak
all the grief we bore.
The nurses kept him comfortable
the aides kept him clean
he was precious in those moments
stripped of all the "mean."

The Priest came to see my dad,
who was a "sinner" all his life.
he abused his family in many ways
he cheated on his wife.
Dad took his hand and asked if God
would forgive him all his sins
he asked, "Will I be forgiven?"
and if God would let him "in?"

The Priest, who was a young man
was tender with my dad
forgiveness? It was absolute
that God already had.
Dad asked again, "Are you sure?"
He had a furrowed brow
the Priest held dad's hand
and said, "Let just pray, right now."

My dad closed his eyes
and my tears fell upon his knees
I saw his muscles loosen
I watched his breathing ease.
The Priest granted "absolution"
my dad was safe to go
on a journey, was predestined
somewhere we couldn't know.

I have thought about that moment,
many times since then
I witnessed a change in Dad
as his life came to an end.
I believe he was forgiven
that love found him where he lay
and it was because of THAT ONE MOMENT
– I can love my dad today.

My heart changed with dad's
as I witnessed what I saw
the anger left his eyes
he lost the tightness in his jaw.
His face became relaxed
no longer tight and drawn
and a few short hours later
my dad was simply gone.

I have a hospice heart.

I TOOK SOME TIME TO GRIEVE TODAY

I took some time to grieve today
I thought about Elke and her spouse
it must seem dark and lonely
without Ron wandering 'round the house.

I remembered our friend Jim
and I thought about Kathleen
her heart was in New York
she was a Staten Island Queen.

I smiled when I thought of Connie
and her "impish" little grin
I saw Carly in her Wheelchair
with two shots of Bombay gin.

I remembered tender John
with one daughter and three sons
I will never forget Dorothy
or her husband's silly puns.

I can't forget Anita and how
she loved her brother, dear
she was ohh so grateful
to have hospice share her tears.

Howard will make me wince
if I think about his loss
he combed her hair each day
'til her bridge was finally crossed.

And Ruby's son, so earnest
as his mom began to die
his dad, Felix, standing strong
fighting tears back in his eyes.

I'm sure I could go on and on
and say more about our friends
who've wandered cross our paths
as they prepared for life to end.

But I think I'll stop right here
and breathe a sigh that's deep
take a moment to let go
and perhaps a pause to weep.

I have a hospice heart.

ABOUT THE AUTHOR

Terry Mills began her writing career in 1970. As a young writer, she wrote two essays resulting in a scholarship for high school and a cash award for books and supplies. She would later win the notice and accolades of her teachers, as well as a creative-writing award. In college, she utilized original poetry in presentations, projects, and papers. Terry was able to speak out on issues of social justice through poignant, or political poetry. In her professional life, Terry has written personal poetry for her patients and families. Terry has presented her work in multiple venues in Phoenix, from coffee houses, bookstores and small listening venues, to story-telling events, poetry contests and Senior Centers. She has facilitated Poetry Workshops and assisted with the poetic expression of participants. Terry has brought poetry readings to rehab centers, retirement communities, group homes and churches. She has a YouTube channel. Terry believes her work is meant to be shared.

BOOK TERRY MILLS TO SPEAK AT YOUR NEXT EVENT!

hospiceheart2018@gmail.com

Made in the USA
San Bernardino, CA
12 January 2019